To my mother, Frances Shapiro —LS

To Sachiko Kimura —HT

It's Time to Give Up Your Pacifier

a transition times book

Lawrence E. Shapiro, Ph.D.
Illustrated by **Hideko Takahashi**

Instant Help Books

Lots of children like you love their pacifiers.

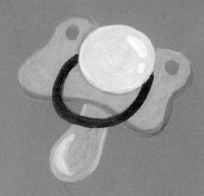

They have names for them like
Binky, Paci, Nitzi, or Boo.

What do you call yours?

You've had your pacifier since you were a baby.

It has calmed you and helped you to sleep.

But now you are
a big kid!

You can do
big-kid things.

Big boys and girls don't need to suck on things like babies do.

Besides, there are plenty of other things you can do with your mouth that are more fun.

You can talk.

You can blow bubbles.

You can eat.

You can stick out your tongue.

You can give kisses.

You can't do any of these with a pacifier in your mouth!

It's time to give up your pacifier so you can do big-kid things!

It's hard to give up
something you love.

**But growing up means finding
new things to make you happy.**

Here is the best way to give up your pacifier. It's as easy as 1 2 3.

1

Leave your pacifier at home when you go out to play.

2

Leave your pacifier
on the bedside table
when you wake up.

3 Leave your pacifier on the bedside table when you go to sleep.

Bye-bye, pacifier.

When you open your
eyes, you will see . . .

Advice for Parents

Dear Parents,

Many parents worry when it's time for their child to give up using a pacifier. They anticipate that their child will have a difficult time—and usually they are right! The happy news is that with a good plan and some firm resolve, your child's crying and complaints will not last more than a few days.

Reading this book with your child will help set the stage for getting rid of the pacifier, but it is still up to you to make it happen. I recommend creating a transition-time plan, and even writing it down. When you write down your plan, you are making a firm commitment to behave in the best possible way for your child. It is also easier to share a written plan with other caregivers.

Most pediatricians recommend giving pacifiers to newborns to help calm them when they fuss. Babies have a sucking instinct, and a pacifier helps satisfy this urge when they are not hungry. But the sucking instinct fades by a child's first birthday, and this is a good time to think about weaning a child off of a pacifier.

A child who is eighteen months old is definitely ready to give up the pacifier entirely. However, many parents wait until children are three or even older—and waiting usually just makes things worse. There are some very good reasons to have your child stop using a pacifier by eighteen months of age.

- **Although pacifiers don't usually cause dental problems, constant use has been associated with upper jaw deformation.**
- **Pacifier use has been linked to an increase in ear infections.**
- **Although some toddlers learn to talk even with a pacifier in their mouth, for most children sucking on a pacifier inhibits speaking.**
- **By age two or three, a child who still uses a pacifier might be teased by other children. More importantly, when children are sucking on a pacifier, it's hard to read their facial expressions accurately, making it more likely that children and adults will react to them in the wrong way.**

Some parents prefer to go cold turkey when it is time for their child to give up using a pacifier. If you do this, you will undoubtedly experience two or three days of your child's displeasure, but then it is over for good.

You can also take a more gradual approach, limiting the use of the pacifier before it is gone for good. If you want to decrease pacifier use slowly, here is what you can do:

Week 1: Tell your child that it is time to stop using the pacifier except at home. Say that soon he or she will not need the pacifier at all.

Week 2: Tell your child that it is time to stop using the pacifier except at bedtime.

Week 3: Tell your child that now he or she is a big kid and does not need a pacifier at all. Throw all of your child's pacifiers away, out of sight of your child. Give your child a special stuffed toy to take to bed in place of the pacifier.

Prepare yourself for three or four days of fussing and crying at bedtime. Don't give in and give your child a pacifier. By the end of the week, your child will no longer need a pacifier.

Whether you go cold turkey or restrict the use of the pacifier slowly, here are some important things to remember:

- **Be consistent. Once you have a good plan, stick to it, and never give the pacifier back to your child once it has been taken away.**

- **Avoid taking the pacifier away at a time of change, such as a move, when a new baby is coming, or at the start of a new school year.**

- **Do not give your child a hard time, even though your child might give you one.**

- **Do not make your child feel bad about wanting the pacifier back.**

Go to our website, www.TransitionTimesBooks.com, for more tips to help your child give up his pacifier.

Different parents use different ways to help their child stop using a pacifier. Some parents tell their child that a Binky Fairy will come while they sleep and take away the pacifier. The Binky Fairy leaves a special stuffed toy, sometimes with a note. Here are some other ways that parents recommend:

- **Break the pacifier by cutting off the nipple. Then tell your child it is broken and needs to be thrown away.**
- **Ask your dentist to tell your child that the pacifier is bad for his or her teeth.**
- **Gradually decrease the places your child uses the pacifier.**
- **Gradually decrease the time your child uses the pacifier.**
- **Give stickers to your child when he or she doesn't use the pacifier.**
- **Dip the pacifier in soapy water so that it will taste bad.**

Whatever method you choose, remember to convey a positive attitude to your child about giving up the pacifier. This is a really important milestone—like using the potty or going to preschool—and you should feel proud and happy to see your child grow. A smile, a hug, and lots of patience is what you and your child need, for now, and for other transition times ahead.

Good luck!

Lawrence Shapiro, Ph.D.

The **transition times** series is designed to help parents understand the importance of addressing developmental issues at the right time and in the right way. Each book addresses a specific transition in the lives of children, when they often need a gentle nudge forward on the road to responsibility and independence. The books provide parents with a way to talk to their children that will hold their interest and make facing life's challenges seem less overwhelming. The books also help parents understand age-appropriate expectations, and give them a simple and clear context to set realistic limits. Reading the books to children will make bumpy transition times just a little bit smoother.

Publisher's Note

An Instant Help Book

Distributed in Canada by Raincoast Books

Text copyright © 2008 by Lawrence Shapiro, Ph.D.
New Harbinger Publications, Inc.
5674 Shattuck Avenue
Oakland, CA 94609
www.newharbinger.com

Illustrations by Hideko Takahashi
Cover and text design by Amy Shoup
Acquired by Tesilya Hanauer
The illustrations were done in acrylic paint on multimedia paper.
This book was typeset in Souvenir BT.

Library of Congress Cataloging-in-Publication Data
Shapiro, Lawrence E.
  It's time to give up your pacifier : a transition time book / Lawrence E. Shapiro.
    p. cm. -- (Transition times)
  ISBN-13: 978-1-57224-585-3 (hardcover : alk. paper)
  ISBN-10: 1-57224-585-9 (hardcover : alk. paper) 1. Toddlers. 2. Pacifiers (Infant care)
3. Habit breaking. 4. Child rearing. I. Title.
  HQ774.5.S53 2008
  649'.6--dc22
                              2008029592

10   09   08

10   9   8   7   6   5   4   3   2   1

First printing